EP Physics/Chemistry Printables: Levels 5-8

This book belongs to:

_____

This book was made for your convenience. It is available for printing from the Easy Peasy All-in-One Homeschool website. It contains all of the printables from Easy Peasy's physics/chemistry course. The instructions for each page are found in the online course.

Easy Peasy All-in-One Homeschool is a free online homeschool curriculum providing high quality education for children around the globe. It provides complete courses for preschool through high school graduation. For EP's curriculum visit allinonehomeschool.com.

EP Physics/Chemistry Printables: Levels 5-8

ISBN: 9781096810308

First Edition: August 2019

Element Lapbook
Pages

| Cut along the outside lines and fold in half. Write the name of the element and information about the element inside the booklet.

Glue this side to the correct periodic table group section. | H

1 |

| Cut along the outside lines and fold in half. Write the name of the element and information about the element inside the booklet.

Glue this side to the correct periodic table group section. | He

2 |

| Cut along the outside lines and fold in half. Write the name of the element and information about the element inside the booklet.

Glue this side to the correct periodic table group section. | C

6 |

Cut along the outside lines and fold in half. Write the name of the element and information about the element inside the booklet. Glue this side to the correct periodic table group section.	O 8
Cut along the outside lines and fold in half. Write the name of the element and information about the element inside the booklet. Glue this side to the correct periodic table group section.	Ne 10
Cut along the outside lines and fold in half. Write the name of the element and information about the element inside the booklet. Glue this side to the correct periodic table group section.	Na 11

Cut along the outside lines and fold in half. Write the name of the element and information about the element inside the booklet. Glue this side to the correct periodic table group section.	 12
Cut along the outside lines and fold in half. Write the name of the element and information about the element inside the booklet. Glue this side to the correct periodic table group section.	Al 13
Cut along the outside lines and fold in half. Write the name of the element and information about the element inside the booklet. Glue this side to the correct periodic table group section.	Si 14

Cut along the outside lines and fold in half. Write the name of the element and information about the element inside the booklet. Glue this side to the correct periodic table group section.	Cl 17
Cut along the outside lines and fold in half. Write the name of the element and information about the element inside the booklet. Glue this side to the correct periodic table group section.	K 19
Cut along the outside lines and fold in half. Write the name of the element and information about the element inside the booklet. Glue this side to the correct periodic table group section.	Ca 20

Cut along the outside lines and fold in half. Write the name of the element and information about the element inside the booklet. Glue this side to the correct periodic table group section.	Fe 26
Cut along the outside lines and fold in half. Write the name of the element and information about the element inside the booklet. Glue this side to the correct periodic table group section.	Ni 28
Cut along the outside lines and fold in half. Write the name of the element and information about the element inside the booklet. Glue this side to the correct periodic table group section.	Cu 29

| Cut along the outside lines and fold in half. Write the name of the element and information about the element inside the booklet. Glue this side to the correct periodic table group section. | Zn 30 |

| Cut along the outside lines and fold in half. Write the name of the element and information about the element inside the booklet. Glue this side to the correct periodic table group section. | Ag 47 |

| Cut along the outside lines and fold in half. Write the name of the element and information about the element inside the booklet. Glue this side to the correct periodic table group section. | Ar 18 |

Cut along the outside lines and fold in half. Write the name of the element and information about the element inside the booklet. Glue this side to the correct periodic table group section.	I 53
Cut along the outside lines and fold in half. Write the name of the element and information about the element inside the booklet. Glue this side to the correct periodic table group section.	Au 79
Cut along the outside lines and fold in half. Write the name of the element and information about the element inside the booklet. Glue this side to the correct periodic table group section.	Pb 82

Periodic Table of the Elements

Group→	1	2	3	4	5	6	7	8	9	10	11	12	13	14	15	16	17	18
Period 1	1 H																	2 He
2	3 Li	4 Be											5 B	6 C	7 N	8 O	9 F	10 Ne
3	11 Na	12 Mg											13 Al	14 Si	15 P	16 S	17 Cl	18 Ar
4	19 K	20 Ca	21 Sc	22 Ti	23 V	24 Cr	25 Mn	26 Fe	27 Co	28 Ni	29 Cu	30 Zn	31 Ga	32 Ge	33 As	34 Se	35 Br	36 Kr
5	37 Rb	38 Sr	39 Y	40 Zr	41 Nb	42 Mo	43 Tc	44 Ru	45 Rh	46 Pd	47 Ag	48 Cd	49 In	50 Sn	51 Sb	52 Te	53 I	54 Xe
6	55 Cs	56 Ba		72 Hf	73 Ta	74 W	75 Re	76 Os	77 Ir	78 Pt	79 Au	80 Hg	81 Tl	82 Pb	83 Bi	84 Po	85 At	86 Rn
7	87 Fr	88 Ra		104 Rf	105 Db	106 Sg	107 Bh	108 Hs	109 Mt	110 Ds	111 Rg	112 Cn	113 Uut	114 Fl	115 Uup	116 Lv	117 Uus	118 Uuo

Lanthanides	57 La	58 Ce	59 Pr	60 Nd	61 Pm	62 Sm	63 Eu	64 Gd	65 Tb	66 Dy	67 Ho	68 Er	69 Tm	70 Yb	71 Lu
Actinides	89 Ac	90 Th	91 Pa	92 U	93 Np	94 Pu	95 Am	96 Cm	97 Bk	98 Cf	99 Es	100 Fm	101 Md	102 No	103 Lr

Worksheet Pages

Changing States of Matter

Use the words in the box to fill in the blanks below.

| 0° cool heat 100° freeze melt 32° condense evaporate 212° |

When you _____ water to _____ C or _____ F, it will _____ to form steam.

When you _____ steam to _____ C or _____ F, it will _____ to form water.

When you _____ ice to _____ C or _____ F, it will _____ to form water.

When you _____ water to _____ C or _____ F, it will _____ to form ice.

Experiment Worksheet

Fill out this worksheet as you work through the experiment.

Question: _____

Hypothesis: _____

_____

Materials: _____

_____

Procedure: _____

_____

_____

_____

_____

Observations/data: _____

_____

_____

_____

_____

Conclusion: _____

_____

_____

Vocabulary

Define these terms.

atom_____

_____

molecule_____

_____

matter_____

_____

state of matter_____

_____

liquid _____

_____

gas_____

_____

solid_____

_____

periodic table_____

_____

Helium

Fill in this chart for helium.

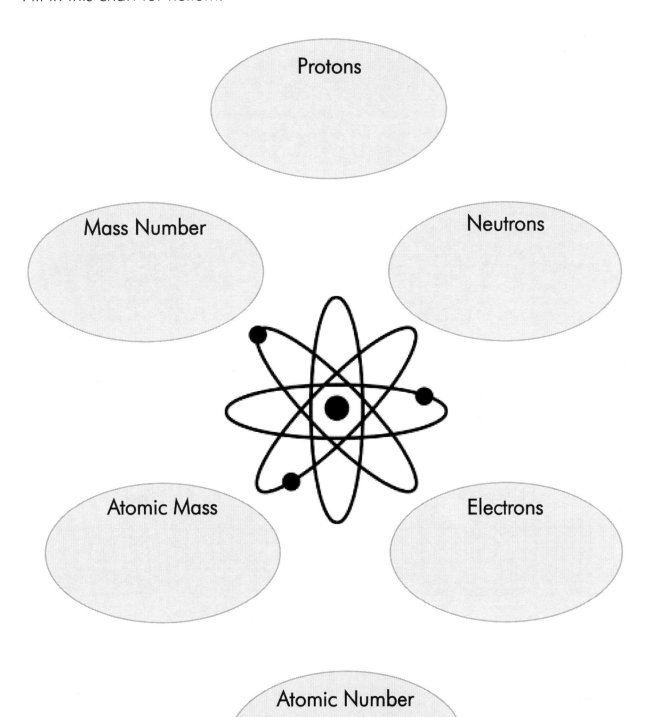

Atoms

Draw 6 protons in the nucleus of the atom and label them with their charge.

Draw 6 neutrons in the nucleus of the atom.

Draw 2 electrons on the inner ring and label them with their charge.

Draw 4 electrons in the outer ring and label them with their charge.

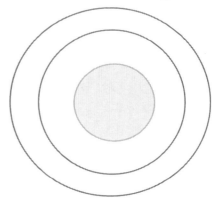

What is the atom?   _____

Fill in the missing information from the chart.

Element	Atomic Mass	Atomic Number	Protons	Neutrons	Electrons
Be	9	4			
N	14				7
Mn		25	25	30	
Au	197				79
Cr		24		28	
H	1		1		

Electrons

Fill out how many protons, neutrons, and electrons each atom has using the information given. Then draw the electrons in each shell, remembering that the first shell can hold 2 electrons, the second can hold 8 electrons, and the third can hold 18 electrons. Finally, answer the questions at the bottom.

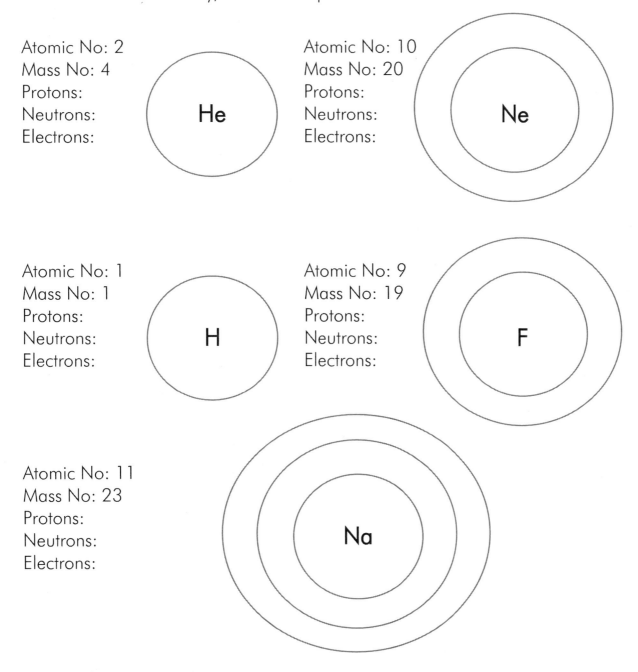

Atomic No: 2
Mass No: 4
Protons:
Neutrons:
Electrons:

Atomic No: 10
Mass No: 20
Protons:
Neutrons:
Electrons:

Atomic No: 1
Mass No: 1
Protons:
Neutrons:
Electrons:

Atomic No: 9
Mass No: 19
Protons:
Neutrons:
Electrons:

Atomic No: 11
Mass No: 23
Protons:
Neutrons:
Electrons:

Which elements would be most likely to lose electrons in a chemical bond? _____

Which elements would be most likely to gain electrons in a chemical bond? _____

Water Cohesion

Use this notebooking page to explain why a cup of water that's too full doesn't spill over immediately.

_____

_____

_____

_____

_____

_____

_____

_____

_____

_____

_____

Chemical Reaction

Use this notebooking page to describe the chemical reaction from the experiment.

_____

_____

_____

_____

_____

_____

_____

_____

_____

_____

_____

Principles of Flight

Use this notebooking page to take notes.

_____

_____

_____

_____

_____

_____

_____

_____

_____

_____

Weight on Other Planets

The surface gravity of each planet relative to earth is in its box. Find out your weight on other planets by writing your weight on earth on the line and multiplying it by the surface gravity of the planet.

Mercury	Venus	Earth
_____	_____	_____
x .38	x .91	x 1

Mars	Jupiter	Saturn
_____	_____	_____
x .38	x 2.36	x 1.05

Uranus	Neptune	Pluto
_____	_____	_____
x .94	x 1.13	x .07

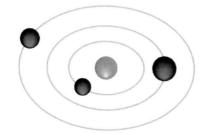

(continued on next page)

Weight, Mass, Gravity

Use this notebooking page to explain how weight, mass, and gravity are connected.

_____

_____

_____

_____

_____

_____

_____

_____

_____

_____

_____

_____

Lesson
37

Experiment Worksheet

Fill out this worksheet as you work through the experiment.

Question: _____

Hypothesis: _____

_____

Materials: _____

_____

Procedure: _____

_____

_____

_____

_____

Observations/data: _____

_____

_____

_____

_____

Conclusion: _____

_____

_____

pH Test

Use this sheet to record your findings.

Objective: to find out if liquids are acid, neutral, or base

Testing	Color	Conclusion
Vinegar	pink	acid

Acids and Bases

Answer the following questions about acids and bases.

What is a characteristic of an acid? _____

_____

What is a characteristic of a base? _____

_____

List some acids: _____

List some bases: _____

What is the pH of a strong acid? _____

What color does a strong acid turn when tested for its pH
level? _____

What is the pH of a strong base? _____

What color does a strong base turn when tested for its pH
level? _____

What atom is abundantly present in an acid? _____

What atom is abundantly present in a base? _____

Chemical Reactions

Fill in the blanks as you watch the video.

1. A chemical reaction is the process of one or more substances

   _____ to form new substances with different properties.

2. In chemical reactions, a new substance is formed from chemicals

   _____ with each other.

3. _____ are substances that enter a chemical reaction,

   while _____ are substances that are produced by a

   chemical reaction.

4. A chemical _____ is an expression using chemical

   symbols to represent a chemical reaction.

5. A plus sign is used to show that substances _____.

6. An _____ is used to show products yielded by reactants.

7. Label the reactants and the products in this chemical equation:

   _____   _____

   ## $2H_2 + O_2 \rightarrow 2H_2O$

8. The law of the _____ of mass says that mass cannot

   be gained or lost in a chemical reaction.

9. The number of _____ of each element must be the same

   before and after a chemical reaction.

10. A _____ reaction is where two or more simple

    substances combine to form a more complex substance.

(continued on next page)

11. A _____ reaction is where a substance breaks down into two or more simple substances.

12. A _____-_____ reaction is where atoms of one element replace atoms of another element in a compound.

13. A _____-_____ reaction is where atoms in two different compounds trade places with each other.

14. Chemical reactions involve _____ being given off or being absorbed.

15. An _____ reaction releases energy and gives off heat.

16. An _____ reaction absorbs energy resulting in the lowering of temperature.

17. Variables such as temperature, surface area, and concentration affect the _____ of chemical reactions, or the speed with which reactants turn into products.

18. The _____ _____ is the amount of material that comes in contact with other reactants.

19. _____ is the amount of substance in a given unit of volume.

20. A _____ is a substance that increases the reaction rate but is not changed by the reaction.

Experiment Worksheet

Fill out this worksheet as you work through the experiment.

Question: _____

Hypothesis: _____

_____

Materials: _____

_____

Procedure: _____

_____

_____

_____

_____

Observations/data: _____

_____

_____

_____

_____

Conclusion: _____

_____

_____

Density Worksheet

Answer the questions about density. You can use a calculator. Remember that **D**ensity = **M**ass / **V**olume. You can reverse that to be V=M/D and M=D*V.

1. A container has a capacity of 1400 milliliters. If the density of ethanol is .789 g/mL, what mass of ether can the bottle hold?

2. 200 grams of a liquid fills a 400 mL container. What is the density of the liquid?

3. If a block of iron measures 1 cm x 2 cm x 3 cm and weighs 47.16 grams, what is its density?

4. The density of mercury is 13.6 g/mL. What is the mass of 10 mL of mercury?

5. If a solution has a density of 2.5 g/mL, how many grams are needed to obtain 10 mL of solution?

6. A piece of silver has a mass of 3360 grams and occupies a volume of 320 cm^3. What is the silver's density?

Define these terms.

Viscosity: _____

_____

_____

_____

Density: _____

_____

_____

_____

Buoyancy: _____

_____

_____

_____

Capillary Action: _____

_____

_____

_____

Endothermic Reaction

Use these sheets to conduct your endothermic and exothermic experiments.

Endothermic Reaction Procedure:

1. Measure 10 ml of vinegar and pour it into a clear container.

2. Place a thermometer in the container. Measure and record the temperature of the vinegar on the chart.

3. Leaving the thermometer in the cup, add ½ teaspoon of baking soda.

4. Watch the thermometer and observe the changes in temperature. When the thermometer stops moving, record the temperature on the chart.

	Temperature
Vinegar without baking soda	
Vinegar with baking soda	
Total change in temperature	
Increase or decrease?	

(continued on next page)

Exothermic Reaction

Exothermic Reaction Procedure:

1. Measure 10 ml of baking soda solution and pour it into a clear container.

2. Place a thermometer in the container. Measure and record the temperature of the baking soda on the chart.

3. Leaving the thermometer in the cup, add ½ teaspoon of calcium chloride.

4. Watch the thermometer and observe the changes in temperature. When the thermometer stops moving, record the temperature on the chart.

5. Now add another 5°C or 10°F to the temperature you achieved. This is your target temperature for your next three trials. Fill it in on the chart in all three columns.

6. Try changing the amount of baking soda solution or calcium chloride in each trial to reach the target temperature.

Trials	As written	1ˢᵗ Trial	2ⁿᵈ Trial	3ʳᵈ Trial
Baking soda solution	10 ml			
Initial temperature				
Calcium chloride	½ tsp			
Final temperature				
Target temperature				
Difference between final and target temperature				

Experiment Worksheet

Fill out this worksheet as you work through the experiment.

Question: _____

Hypothesis: _____

_____

Materials: _____

_____

Procedure: _____

_____

_____

_____

_____

Observations/data: _____

_____

_____

_____

_____

Conclusion: _____

_____

_____

Electricity Timeline

Use the blanks to fill in a timeline of electricity events you want to remember. Be sure to include the year.

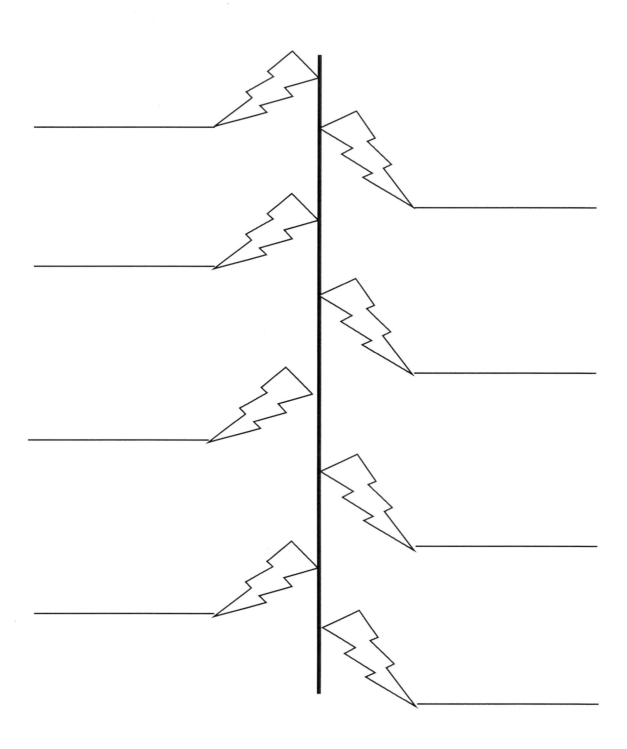

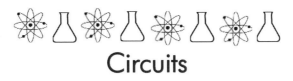

Circuits

Write any notes about circuits from your assignments today.

_____

_____

_____

Explain an open circuit.
Draw an example.

_____

_____

_____

_____

_____

Explain a closed circuit.
Draw an example.

_____

_____

_____

_____

_____

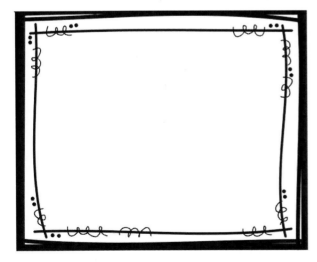

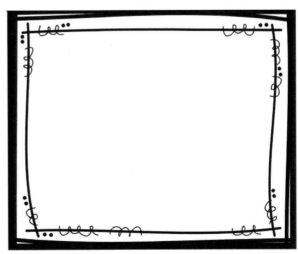

Static Electricity

Do the following experiment and take notes on what happens and why.

Materials: two balloons, two 3-foot pieces of string, tape.

Procedure: Blow up the balloons and tie the strings to the ends. Hang them beside each other in a doorway so that they are close but not touching each other. From their hanging position, rub each balloon on your hair and then let go. Record what happens.

_____

_____

_____

_____

The balloons should have pushed away from each other. Why did that happen? The balloons became similarly charged. What do you know about like charges?

_____

_____

_____

_____

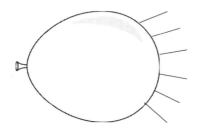 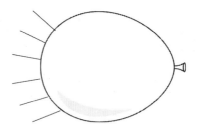

Magnets

What are magnets?

_____

_____

_____

_____

What have you learned about magnets? Make notes here.

_____

_____

_____

_____

AC/DC Power

What is the difference between AC and DC power? Fill in what each letter stands for and then explain what the difference is.

A _____

C _____

D _____

C _____

_____

_____

_____

_____

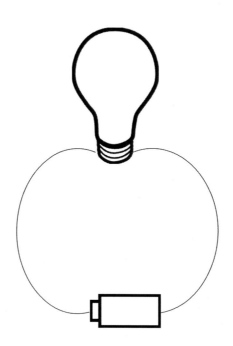

GFCI Outlet

What is a GFCI outlet? What do the letters stand for?

G _____

F _____

C _____

I _____

What are benefits of GFCI outlets? Where are they used?

_____

_____

_____

_____

Vocabulary

Define these terms.

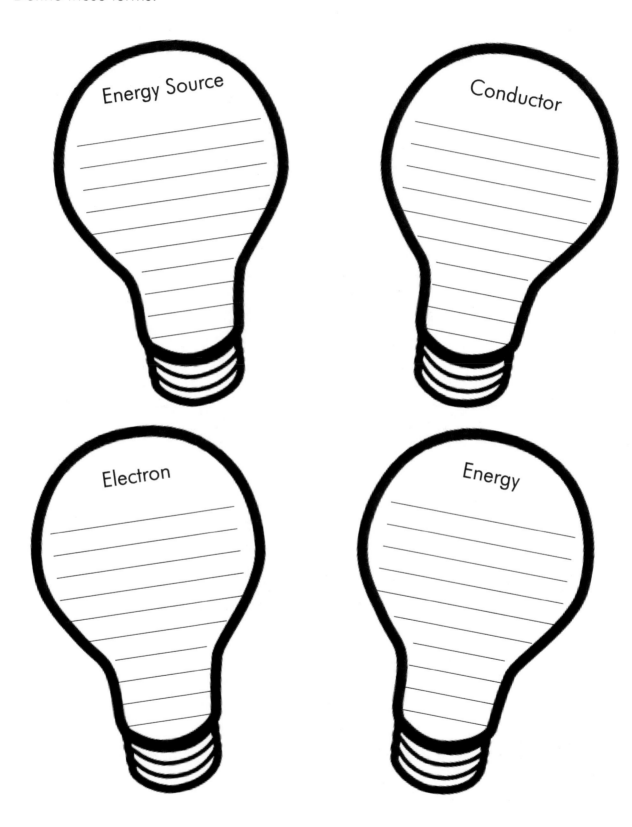

Energy Source

Conductor

Electron

Energy

Experiment Worksheet

Fill out this worksheet as you work through the experiment.

Question: _____

Hypothesis: _____

_____

Materials: _____

_____

Procedure: _____

_____

_____

_____

_____

Observations/data: _____

_____

_____

_____

_____

Conclusion: _____

_____

_____

Magnetism

Define these terms.

AC _____

_____

domain _____

_____

electromagnet_____

_____

electron_____

_____

geographic pole_____

_____

magnetic field_____

_____

Electromagnets

Answers these questions about electromagnets.

An electromagnet runs on _____.

The strength of an electromagnet **can / cannot** be changed.

In an electromagnet, electric current produces a _____

_____.

The magnetic field of an electromagnet can be strengthened

by wrapping this around a core. _____.

As the current in an electromagnet strengthens, the magnetic

field gets **stronger / weaker**.

An electric current flowing towards you will create a magnetic

field that will circulate **clockwise / counter-clockwise**.

Magnetic Grippers

Draw a gripper in action. Explain what's happening in your picture.

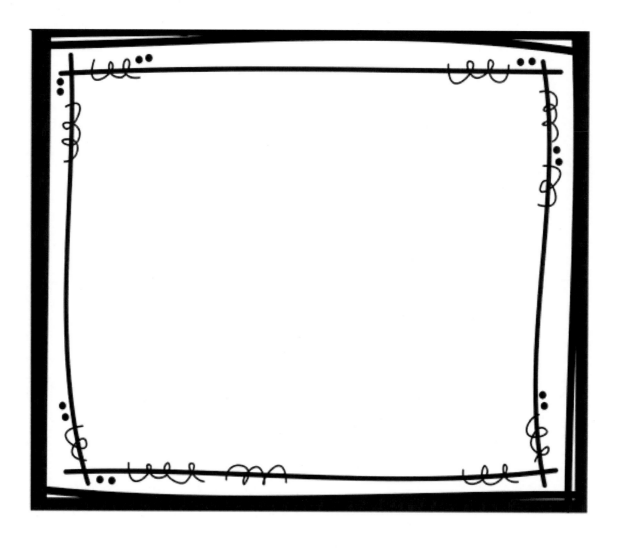

_____

_____

_____

_____

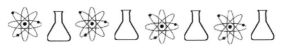

Earth's Magnetic Field

What creates the Earth's magnetic field?

_____
_____
_____
_____

What does a compass needle do?

_____
_____ .
_____
_____ .
_____

Are the magnetic and geographic poles the same?

_____
_____
_____
_____

Electricity Conductors

Use this sheet to record your findings.

Objective: to find out if objects conduct or carry electricity.

Testing	Conductor	Not Conductor
water	X	

Chemistry Review

Define these terms as you work through lessons 96-99.

Lesson 96:

physical change_____

_____

ionic bond_____

_____

solubility_____

_____

Lesson 97:

solute_____

_____

solvent _____

_____

Lesson 98:

chemical reactions_____

_____

(continued on next page)

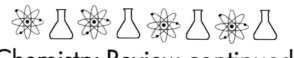

Lesson 98 continued:
concentrations_____

_____

Lesson 99:
freezing_____

_____

heat_____

_____

evaporation_____

_____

condensation_____

_____

temperature_____

_____

Ionic Bonds

Write a short description beside each picture to show the process of ionic bonding. The first one is done for you.

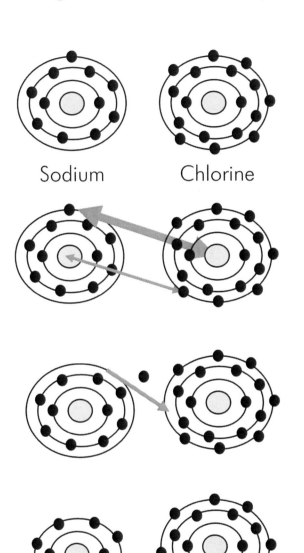

Sodium   Chlorine

An atom of sodium and an atom of chlorine are near each other.

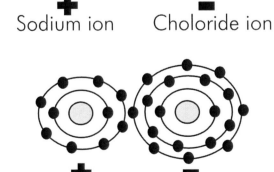

Sodium ion   Choloride ion

Sodium Choloride (NaCl)

Lewis Dot Diagrams

Answer the following questions about Lewis dot diagrams.

Compare the energy level diagrams to the Lewis dot diagrams.

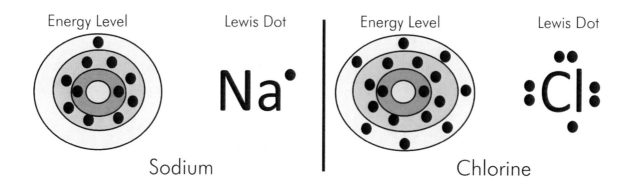

Energy Level   Lewis Dot   Energy Level   Lewis Dot

Na°   :Cl:

Sodium   Chlorine

What do you notice about the dots in each diagram? _____

_____

_____

Energy Level   Lewis Dot   Energy Level   Lewis Dot

H°   He•

Hydrogen   Helium

Why are the number of dots associated with hydrogen and helium the

same on each type of diagram? _____

_____

(continued on next page)

Compare the energy level diagram for a covalent bond in the hydrogen molecule H_2 with the Lewis dot diagram of the same bond.

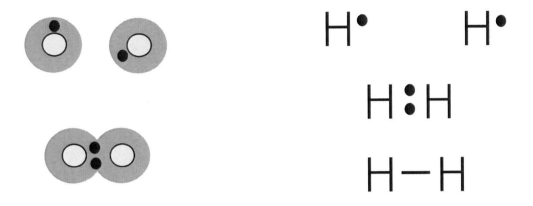

H•   H•

H:H

H—H

What do the two dots represent between the Hs? _____

What do the two lines represent? _____

Draw a Lewis dot diagram for the covalent bond of two hydrogen atoms to one oxygen atom in a water molecule. Use dots in the first diagram and lines in the second.

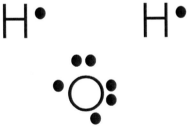

Force

For the following pictures, tell whether the force at work is a push or a pull.

 _____

  _____

_____

Circle the answer that fits with each picture.

←100 n   100 n →   ←100 n   200 n →

The forces shown are _____ forces.

  pushing   pulling   pushing   pulling

The forces shown are _____.

  working together   opposite   working together   opposite

The forces are _____.

  equal   not equal   equal   not equal

The forces _____ balance each other.

  do   do not   do   do not

The resultant force is _____.

100 n left   100 n right   zero   100 n left   100 n right   zero

There _____ motion.

is   is not   is   is not

Force

Sometimes force is shown as a **vector**. The dot shows where the force begins. The length shows the amount of force. The arrow shows the direction of the force. This vector shows a force of 3 n to the right.

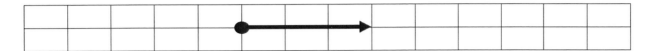

Fill in the chart with the information about the vectors below. Each square is 1 n.

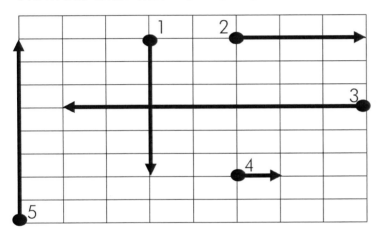

	Force	Direction
1		
2		
3		
4		
5		

Draw the following vectors on the grid below. 1) 7 n right; 2) 3 n up; 3) 4 n down; 4) 6 n left; 5) 1 n down.

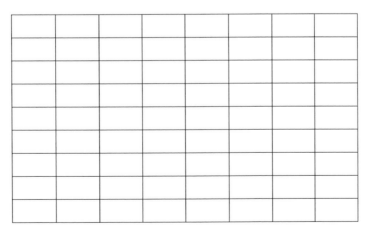

(continued on next page)

Here are two more examples of vectors showing force. The first chart shows two forces acting in opposite directions. One force is 5 n to the left. One force is 3 n to the right. The resultant force is 2 n to the left as shown.

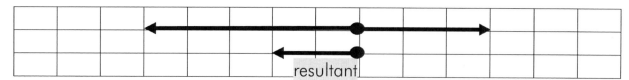

The second chart shows two forces acting in the same direction. One force is 1 n to the right. One force is 4 n to the right. The resultant force is 5 n to the right as shown.

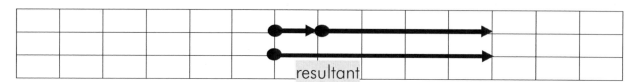

Draw the resultant vector for each set of vectors below. Then fill in the chart for each set. The first one is done for you.

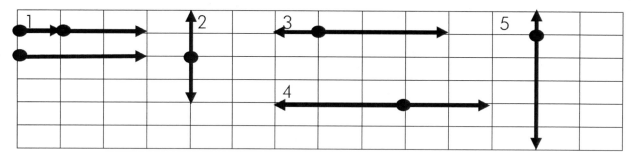

	Original forces	Resultant force
1	1 n right, 2 n right	3 n right
2		
3		
4		
5		

Newton's Laws of Motion

Write about Newton's three Laws of Motion.

1st Law:

Inertia

_____

_____

_____

_____

2nd Law:

Acceleration

_____

_____

_____

_____

3rd Law:

Action/Reaction

_____

_____

_____

_____

Newton's Laws of Motion

Write about your demonstration of each law on the lines.

1ˢᵗ Law: Inertia

An object in motion tends to stay in motion; an object at rest tends to stay at rest.

_____

_____

_____

_____

2ⁿᵈ Law: Acceleration

The acceleration of an object is directly related to the force applied and inversely related to the object's mass ($F=MA$).

_____

_____

_____

_____

3ʳᵈ Law: Action/Reaction

For every action there is an equal and opposite reaction.

_____

_____

_____

Vocabulary

Fill in the definition for each word, draw a picture of it, and tell what it reminds you of.

Speed

Definition _____

_____

Reminds me of _____

_____

Definition _____

_____

Reminds me of _____

_____

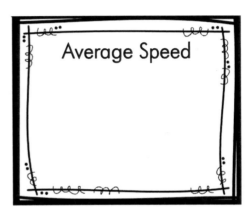

Average Speed

Instantaneous Speed

Definition _____

_____

Reminds me of _____

_____

Definition _____

_____

Reminds me of _____

_____

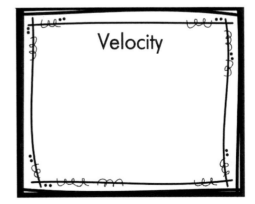

Velocity

Newton's Laws of Motion

For each given scenario, write in the blank whether it illustrates Newton's first, second, or third Law of Motion.

1st Law: Inertia	2nd Law: Acceleration	3rd Law: Action/Reaction

My family went on a vacation. We strapped our luggage to the top of the van. One suitcase apparently wasn't under the strap, and the first time my dad hit the brakes hard, the suitcase went flying forward and spilled clothes all over the highway!

_____

A bird was flapping his wings. Each time it pushed its wings down, the bird would go up higher in the air.

_____

William was riding a high speed roller coaster that took a banked turn to the right, and he ended up with a bruise on his left shoulder.

_____

My brother was lifting a box labeled "books." He didn't know my mom had already emptied the box, so he heaved on it, and it went flying through the air. We all had a good laugh.

_____

Jaylen was rowing a canoe. Every time she pushed the oar backward, the boat would propel forward.

_____

Connor was playing baseball in his yard. He noticed that no matter how hard he swung, he couldn't hit the real baseball as far as he could hit the foam one.

_____

Simple Machines

Use this page to draw examples of these simple machines as they are assigned.

Inclined plane

Wedge

Lever

Screw

Wheel and axle

Pulley

Experiment Worksheet

Fill out this worksheet as you work through the experiment.

Question: _____

Hypothesis: _____

_____

Materials: _____

_____

Procedure: _____

_____

_____

_____

_____

Observations/data: _____

_____

_____

_____

_____

Conclusion: _____

_____

_____

Element Go Fish

Carefully tear out these pages and cut out the cards (there are 3 sets of 18 cards). Use them to play a game of element "Go Fish." Ask any information on the card to learn more about the elements as you play. You need 3 cards for a set.

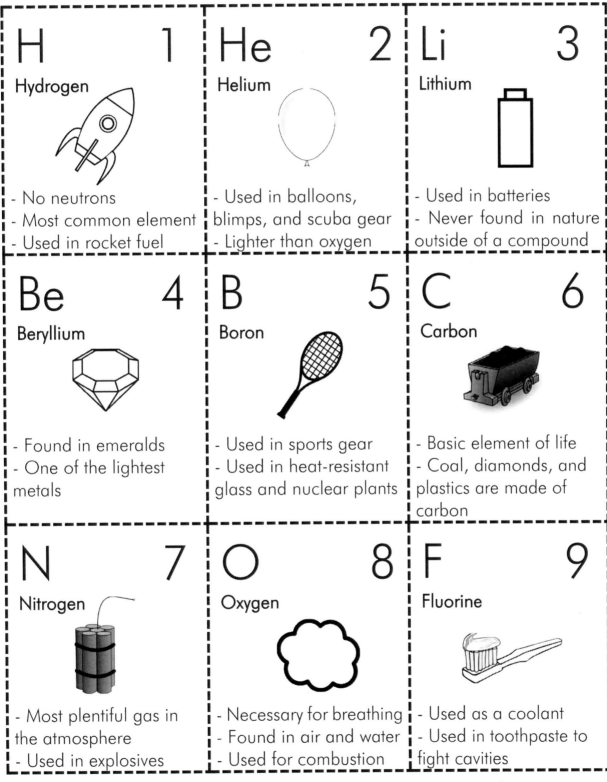

H 1
Hydrogen
- No neutrons
- Most common element
- Used in rocket fuel

He 2
Helium
- Used in balloons, blimps, and scuba gear
- Lighter than oxygen

Li 3
Lithium
- Used in batteries
- Never found in nature outside of a compound

Be 4
Beryllium
- Found in emeralds
- One of the lightest metals

B 5
Boron
- Used in sports gear
- Used in heat-resistant glass and nuclear plants

C 6
Carbon
- Basic element of life
- Coal, diamonds, and plastics are made of carbon

N 7
Nitrogen
- Most plentiful gas in the atmosphere
- Used in explosives

O 8
Oxygen
- Necessary for breathing
- Found in air and water
- Used for combustion

F 9
Fluorine
- Used as a coolant
- Used in toothpaste to fight cavities

(continued on next page)

Element Go Fish

Ne 10 Neon OPEN - Used in lights, lasers - Never bonds to other elements	**Na** 11 Sodium Salt - Bonds with chlorine to make table salt - Never found alone	**Mg** 12 Magnesium - Necessary for plants and animals - Found in sparklers
Al 13 Aluminum - Used in airplanes for its weight and strength - Used in foil, cables	**Si** 14 Silicon ROM - Found in sand, stone, and soil - Used in computer chips	**P** 15 Phosphorus - Used in matches, detergents, fertilizers - Found in bones
S 16 Sulfur - Found in matches, fireworks, egg yolks - Creates air pollution	**Cl** 17 Chlorine - Combines with hydrogen to digest food - Used in swimming pools	**Ar** 18 Argon - Found in light bulbs - Does not react or bond with any other element

(continued on next page)

Element Go Fish

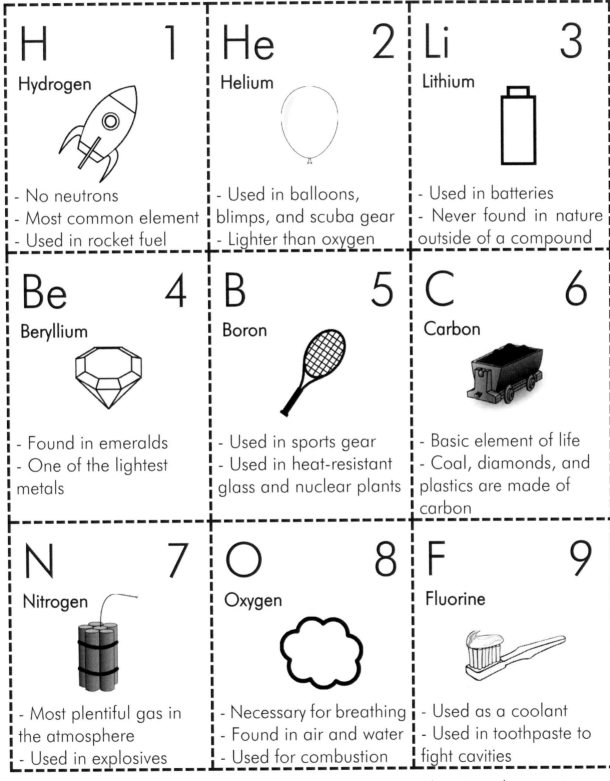

H 1 Hydrogen
- No neutrons
- Most common element
- Used in rocket fuel

He 2 Helium
- Used in balloons, blimps, and scuba gear
- Lighter than oxygen

Li 3 Lithium
- Used in batteries
- Never found in nature outside of a compound

Be 4 Beryllium
- Found in emeralds
- One of the lightest metals

B 5 Boron
- Used in sports gear
- Used in heat-resistant glass and nuclear plants

C 6 Carbon
- Basic element of life
- Coal, diamonds, and plastics are made of carbon

N 7 Nitrogen
- Most plentiful gas in the atmosphere
- Used in explosives

O 8 Oxygen
- Necessary for breathing
- Found in air and water
- Used for combustion

F 9 Fluorine
- Used as a coolant
- Used in toothpaste to fight cavities

(continued on next page)

Element Go Fish

Ne 10	Na 11	Mg 12
Neon	Sodium	Magnesium
OPEN	Salt	
- Used in lights, lasers - Never bonds to other elements	- Bonds with chlorine to make table salt - Never found alone	- Necessary for plants and animals - Found in sparklers
Al 13	Si 14	P 15
Aluminum	Silicon	Phosphorus
ROM		
- Used in airplanes for its weight and strength - Used in foil, cables	- Found in sand, stone, and soil - Used in computer chips	- Used in matches, detergents, fertilizers - Found in bones
S 16	Cl 17	Ar 18
Sulfur	Chlorine	Argon
- Found in matches, fireworks, egg yolks - Creates air pollution	- Combines with hydrogen to digest food - Used in swimming pools	- Found in light bulbs - Does not react or bond with any other element

(continued on next page)

Element Go Fish

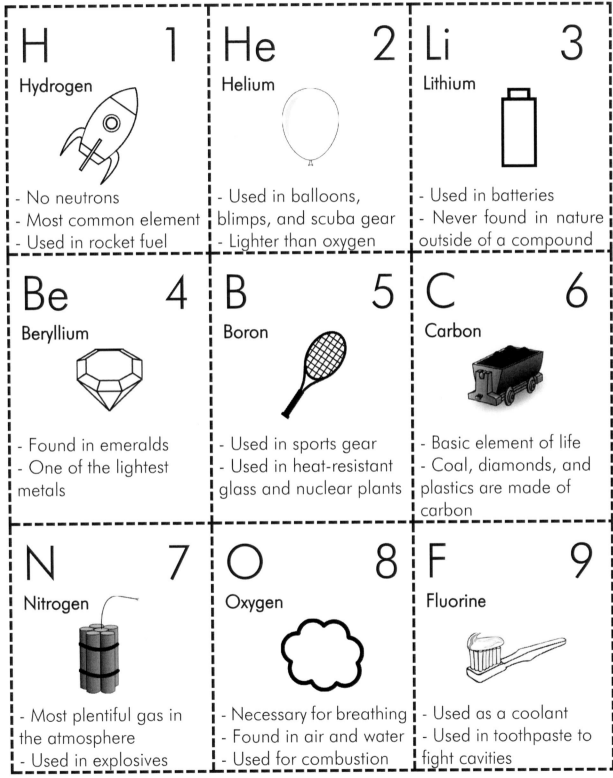

H   1

Hydrogen

- No neutrons
- Most common element
- Used in rocket fuel

He   2

Helium

- Used in balloons, blimps, and scuba gear
- Lighter than oxygen

Li   3

Lithium

- Used in batteries
- Never found in nature outside of a compound

Be   4

Beryllium

- Found in emeralds
- One of the lightest metals

B   5

Boron

- Used in sports gear
- Used in heat-resistant glass and nuclear plants

C   6

Carbon

- Basic element of life
- Coal, diamonds, and plastics are made of carbon

N   7

Nitrogen

- Most plentiful gas in the atmosphere
- Used in explosives

O   8

Oxygen

- Necessary for breathing
- Found in air and water
- Used for combustion

F   9

Fluorine

- Used as a coolant
- Used in toothpaste to fight cavities

(continued on next page)

Element Go Fish

Ne 10	Na 11	Mg 12
Neon	Sodium	Magnesium
OPEN	Salt	
- Used in lights, lasers - Never bonds to other elements	- Bonds with chlorine to make table salt - Never found alone	- Necessary for plants and animals - Found in sparklers
Al 13	Si 14	P 15
Aluminum	Silicon	Phosphorus
	ROM	
- Used in airplanes for its weight and strength - Used in foil, cables	- Found in sand, stone, and soil - Used in computer chips	- Used in matches, detergents, fertilizers - Found in bones
S 16	Cl 17	Ar 18
Sulfur	Chlorine	Argon
- Found in matches, fireworks, egg yolks - Creates air pollution	- Combines with hydrogen to digest food - Used in swimming pools	- Found in light bulbs - Does not react or bond with any other element

Experiment Worksheet

Fill out this worksheet as you work through the experiment.

Question: _____

Hypothesis: _____

_____

Materials: _____

_____

Procedure: _____

_____

_____

_____

_____

Observations/data: _____

_____

_____

_____

_____

Conclusion: _____

_____

_____

Research Notes

Use these pages to make notes on your topic.

Topic:_____

Resource 1:_____

Info:_____   Info:_____

Info:_____   Info:_____

Info:_____   Info:_____

Resource 2:_____

Info:_____   Info:_____

Info:_____   Info:_____

Info:_____   Info:_____

Resource 3:_____

Info:_____   Info:_____

Info:_____   Info:_____

Info:_____   Info:_____

Resource 4:_____

Info:_____   Info:_____

Info:_____   Info:_____

Info:_____   Info:_____

Resource 5:_____

Info:_____   Info:_____

Info:_____   Info:_____

Info:_____   Info:_____

Resource 6:_____

Info:_____   Info:_____

Info:_____   Info:_____

Info:_____   Info:_____

Resource 7:_____

Info:_____   Info:_____

Info:_____   Info:_____

Info:_____   Info:_____

Resource 8:_____

Info:_____   Info:_____

Info:_____   Info:_____

Info:_____   Info:_____

Resource 9:_____

Info:_____   Info:_____

Info:_____   Info:_____

Info:_____   Info:_____

Science Report Checklist

Use this checklist to help you as you finish up your science project. Aim for a checkmark in each box.

Research
- ☐ Facts
- ☐ Sources
- ☐ Bibliography

Project
- ☐ 3D
- ☐ Neat
- ☐ Teaches all about your topic; shows off all you learned
- ☐ Self-explanatory: someone could look at it and understand what it's all about without you explaining it to them
- ☐ Bibliography displayed with project

Experiment
- ☐ Demonstrates your topic
- ☐ Neatly written up with all parts of the experiment worksheet
- ☐ Able to be done over and over with the same results

Demonstration
- ☐ Clearly state what your project is about
- ☐ Tell about what they will learn from your project
- ☐ Explain how the experiment relates to your topic
- ☐ Demonstrate the experiment
- ☐ State your conclusion
- ☐ Ask if anyone has questions

Made in United States
North Haven, CT
08 October 2021